Sister Dear

CELEBRATING OUR SHARED LIVES

Illustrations Acknowledgments:
Art Resource/Erich Lessing: 40
Fine Art Images, Inc.: Cover, 7, 17, 24-25, 57, 61, 62
Fine Art Photographic Library, Ltd.: 9, 14-15, 22, 30, 33, 42-43, 44
Koechel Peterson: 21
Sotheby's: 46-47
Thomas L. Cathey: 5, 10, 29, 54
Wood River Gallery: 27, 36-37, 49, 52-53

ISBN: 1-57051-117-05

Cover/Interior:
Koechel Peterson & Associates, Minneapolis, MN

Printed in USA

To My
Dear Sister...

In all your caring
and sharing

Love,
Connie

Cherished Moments
Gift Books

A Basket of Friends

A Celebration of Christmas

A Feast of Friendship

Friends of a Feather

Joined at the Heart

Leaves of Gold

Merry Christmas With Love

Dear Mom

Seeds of Kindness

Sister Dear

Strength for a Man's Heart

Sweet Rose of Friendship

Tea for Two

Where Angels Dwell

Sister Dear

Compiled by Rhonda S. Hogan

Brownlow

A sister is someone with whom you can be yourself and tell your innermost secrets to. A sister is someone whom you can go to for advice, when a mother's or father's advice just wouldn't do. With a sister, you can shed the armor that the world sees and say what is truly on your heart. She will understand when no one else does.

With a sister you can let out a deep sigh of relief, and tell all your little vanities, your secrets, your hates and loves, and she will loyally keep them within her heart.

You can abuse her, neglect her, tolerate her; but best of all, you can love her deeply. You can weep with her, laugh with her, pray with her. And through it all she knows and loves you.

But while friends may come and go, the truly best thing about being sisters is that there is no physical distance that can separate the love and memories you have together. And the knowledge that you always have someone to hold your hand, pat your back, and be there at a moment's notice.

RHONDA S. HOGAN

Listen to your father's instruction
and do not forsake your mother's teaching.

PROVERBS 1:8

⁓⁓⁓

There is space within sisterhood
for likeness and difference,
for the subtle differences
that challenge and delight.

CHRISTINE DOWNING

⁓⁓⁓

No one knows you like a person
with whom you've shared a childhood.

ALICE HOFFMAN

I think a sister's love is idealized as perfect, unshakable. We all want it, even if we don't have a sister.

LINDSEY DOREN

There are seekers of wisdom
and seekers of wealth,
I seek thy company so that I may sing.

RABINDRANATH TAGORE

I am not sure that Earth is round
Nor that the sky is really blue.
The tale of why the apples fall
May or may not be true.
I do not know what makes the tides
Nor what tomorrow's world may do,
But I have certainty enough
For I am sure of you.

AMELIA JOSEPHINE BURR

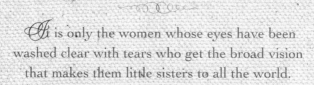

It is only the women whose eyes have been
washed clear with tears who get the broad vision
that makes them little sisters to all the world.

DOROTHY DIX

Each woman has a choice in life;
she may approach it as a creator or critic,
a lover or a hater; a giver or a taker.

UNKNOWN

There is essential meanness in the wish to
get the better of anyone. The only competition
worthy of a wise woman is with herself.

MRS. JAMESON

A kindhearted woman gains respect.

PROVERBS 11:16

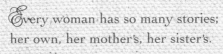

Every woman has so many stories;
her own, her mother's, her sister's.

MARILYN FRENCH

A sister is both your mirror —
and your opposite.

ELIZABETH FISHEL

I cannot deny that now I am without
your company I feel not that I am
deprived of a very dear sister, but
that I have lost half of myself.

BEATRICE D'ESTE

(*Are* we not like two volumes of one book?)

MARCELINE DESBORDES-VALMORE

Sisters — So Much We Share

Growing up, sisters
really do share so much.
They share the same memories,
the same household chores,
the same holiday traditions,
the same relatives,
the same clothes,
and often the same room.

And while time and age
give to each sister
some new experiences,
even these get "shared"
as one story after another
comes tumbling out when
they get together.

But ultimately,
sisters share more than
just time and space together;
they share their hearts.

CAROLINE BROWNLOW

For there is no friend like a sister,

In calm or stormy weather,

To cheer one on the tedious way,

To fetch one if one goes astray,

To lift one if one totters down,

To strengthen whilst one stands.

CHRISTINA ROSSETTI

And God Created Sisters

It wasn't on the first day of creation,

Or on any of those first six days,

But God did create sisters and

They are thereby special.

CAROLINE BROWNLOW

The course of human history is determined,
not by what happens in the skies,
but by what takes place in our hearts.

SIR ARTHUR KEITH

Kind words can be short and easy to speak
but their echoes are truly endless.

MOTHER TERESA

*Nothing is
impossible
to a valiant
heart.*

JEANNE D' ALBRET

The desire to be and have a sister
is a primitive and profound one.

ELIZABETH FISHEL

No matter how old a mother is, she watches her
middle-aged children for signs of improvement.

FLORIDA SCOTT MAXWELL

On thee my soul shall own combined,
the sister and the friend.

CATHERINE KILLIGREW

But the eyes are blind. One must look with the heart.

ANTOINE DE SAINT-EXUPERY

She wore age so gracefully, so carelessly,
that there was a sacred beauty about
her faded cheek more lovely and lovable than
all the bloom of her youth. Happy woman!
Who was not afraid of growing old.

DINAH MARIA MULOCK CRAIK

The Seven Ages of Women

The seven ages of women are:
The first age is a baby,
Then an infant,
Then a miss,
Then she's a young woman,
a young woman,
a young woman,
. a young woman.

Gentle ladies, you will remember till old age
what we did together in our brilliant youth!

SAPPHO

The family whose members work together succeeds.

ELBERT HUBBARD

Where love is there is no labor;
and if there be labor, that labor is loved.

AUSTIN

What do we live for, if it is not to make
life less difficult for each other?

GEORGE ELIOT

One cannot speak enough of the virtues,
the dangers, the power of shared laughter.

FRANÇOISE SAGAN

When sisters are near, hearts abound in love.

CAROLINE BROWNLOW

A sister is a friend.

KAONDE PROVERB

I have made you and I will carry you;
I will sustain you and I will rescue you.

ISAIAH 46:4

The tie of a sister is near and dear indeed.

CHARLOTTE BRONTË

Being with you is like walking on a very clear morning —
definitely the sensation of belonging there.

E. B. WHITE

Sisters, if they be true to the name, have no solitary
joys or sorrows. Sisters cannot help but share them all.

The heart is like a treasure chest
That's filled with souvenirs.
It's there we keep the memories
We gather through the years.

UNKNOWN

To get the full value of joy you must have somebody to divide it with.

MARK TWAIN

To My Sister

My sister! ('tis a wish of mine)
Now that our morning meal is done,
Make haste, your morning task resign;
Come forth and feel the sun.

One moment now may give us more
Than years of toiling reason;
Our minds shall drink at every pore
The spirit of the season.

Then come, my Sister! Come, I pray,
With speed put on your woodland dress;
And bring no book; for this one day
We'll give to idleness.

WILLIAM WORDSWORTH

Garments of Love

Clothe yourselves with

compassion, kindness, humility,

gentleness and patience.

Bear with each other and forgive

whatever grievances you may have.

Forgive as the Lord forgave you.

And over all these virtues put on love,

which binds them all together

in perfect unity.

COLOSSIANS 3:12-14

To Anna

Sister, dear, when you are lonely,

Longing for your distant home,

And the images of loved ones

Warmly to your heart shall come,

Then, mid tender thoughts and fancies,

Let one fond voice say to thee,

"Ever when your heart is heavy,

Anna, dear, then think of me."

Think how we two have together

Journeyed onward day by day,

Joys and sorrows ever sharing,

While the swift years roll away.

Then may all the sunny hours

Of our youth rise up to thee,

And when your heart is light and happy,

Anna, dear, then think of me.

LOUISA MAY ALCOTT TO HER SISTER, ANNA

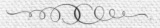

Often, in old age,

they become each other's chosen
and most happy companions.
In addition to their shared
memories of childhood and of their
relationship to each other's children,
they share memories of the same home,
the same homemaking style,
and the same small prejudices
about housekeeping that carry
the echoes of their mother's voice.

MARGARET MEAD

A woman should always stand by a woman.

EURIPIDES

*I*ntimacies between women
often go backwards,
beginning in revelations
and ending in small talk.

ELIZABETH BOWEN

A perfect sister I am not,
but I'm thankful for the ones I've got.

A family is a circle of friends who love you.

ANONYMOUS

Just in case I never told you,
I'm grateful to have you
for my sister, my friend.

CAROLINE BROWNLOW

Sisterly love is, of all sentiments,
the most abstract.

UGO BETTI

A ministering angel shall my sister be.

WILLIAM SHAKESPEARE

A sister is a gift from God, sent from above
to make life worthwhile here below.

My sister! With that thrilling word
Let thoughts unnumbered wildly spring!
What echoes in my heart are stirred,
While thus I touch the trembling string.

MARGARET DAVIDSON

She had come to be a friend and
companion such as few possessed —
intelligent, well-informed, useful, gentle,
knowing all the ways of the family,
interested in all its concerns, and
peculiarly interested in Emma,
in every pleasure, every scheme of hers;
one to whom Emma could speak
every thought as it arose, and she
had such an affection for her
as could never find fault.

JANE AUSTEN

My heart has just been called back to the time
when we used to sit with our arms around
each other at the sunset hour and talk and talk
of our friends and our homes and of ten thousand
subjects of mutual interest until both our hearts felt
warmer and lighter for the pure communion of spirit.

ANTOINETTE LOUISA BROWN

My sister Emily loved the moors. Flowers brighter
than the rose bloomed in the blackest of
the heath for her; out of a sullen hollow in a
livid hill-side, her mind could make an Eden.
She found in the bleak solitude many and dear delights;
and not the least and best-loved was liberty.
Liberty was the breath of Emily's nostrils.

CHARLOTTE BRONTË

As Jesus and his disciples were on their way,
he came to a village where a woman named Martha
opened her home to him. She had a sister called Mary,
who sat at the Lord's feet listening to what he said.
But Martha was distracted by all the preparations
that had to be made. She came to him and asked,
"Lord, don't you care that my sister has left me to
do the work by myself? Tell her to help me!"

"Martha, Martha," the Lord answered, "you are
worried and upset about many things, but only
one thing is needed. Mary has chosen what is better,
and it will not be taken away from her."

Luke 10:38-42

Sister Dear —
I will give you
as much as I can.
If you will show me
how much more to give
then I will give more.
I can only give as much
as you need to receive
or allow me to give.
If you receive all I can give
then my love is
endless and fulfilled.
If you receive a portion
of my love then I will give
others the balance
I am capable of giving.
I must give all that I have
being what I am.

Dear Sister,

Your kind letter I reciev'd today and am greatly rejoiced to (hear) you are all so well. I was very uneasy at not hearing from you, indeed my dear Sister the Winter never seem'd so tedious to me in the World. I daily count the days between this and the time I may probably see you. I could never feel so comfortable as I at present do, if I thought I should spend another Winter here. Indeed my Sister I cannot bear the thought of staying here so far from all my Friends if Mr. Cranch can do as well nigher. I would give a great deal only to know I was within Ten Miles of you if I could not see you. Our children will never seem so natural to each other as if they liv'd where they could see one another oftener....

LETTER FROM MARY SMITH CRANCH
TO HER SISTER, ABIGAIL ADAMS

In the effort to give good and comforting answers
to the young questioners whom we love, we very often
arrive at good and comforting answers for ourselves.

RUTH GOODE

According to popular myth, sisters exist on the
same side of the closed door, sharing teddy bears
and secrets in the privacy of a common bedroom.

MARIANNE PAUL

A sister
is a friend
who listens
with her heart.

Friends, Brothers and Sisters

The Bible says that friends are supposed to love all the time, and that a brother is born for adversity. Well, God knows my brother has certainly given me a lot of adversity. But maybe that's not what it meant.

But what about a sister? What is a sister born for? My sister was born to be the rock of our family. Even before Mother died and Daddy got old, she was the one we depended on. She was the one who always sent the special cards on my birthday—and every other occasion. She loved cards and holidays and family times. She was the one who made sure our little brother didn't get left out of the family gatherings. She was the one who showed me what women of faith look like; she put skin and flesh and life on those old stories of women in the Bible. She taught me how to live. She made me proud of our family.

CAROLINE BROWNLOW

Beauty, Good, and Knowledge
are three sisters
That dote upon each other,
friend to man,
Living together under the same roof,
And never can be
sunder'd without tears.

ALFRED, LORD TENNYSON

A home is the
total contribution of love
on the part of each one
dwelling within it.

ANNE PANNELL

Sisters is probably the most
competitive relationship within the family,
but once the sisters are grown,
it becomes the strongest relationship.

MARGARET MEAD

The family whose members
work together succeeds.

ELBERT HUBBARD

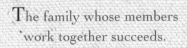

Disagreements have been part of
our relationship—along with forgiveness—
as we are totally different personalities
and love always remains.

CLAUDETTE RENNER

When I was a child
I talked like a child, I thought like a child,
I reasoned like a child. Now that I am grown,
I have put away childish ways.

1 CORINTHIANS 13:11

Letter of Elizabeth Barrett Browning to Her Sisters

I thank and bless you my dearest Henrietta
and Arabel...my own dearest kindest sisters! —
what I suffered in reaching Orleans, —
at last holding all these letters in my hands,
can only be measured by my deep gratitude to you,
and by the tears and kisses I spent upon
every line of what you wrote to me...
dearest kindest that you are.

My thoughts cling to you all,
and will not leave their hold.
Dearest Henrietta and Arabel
let me be as ever and forever.

YOUR FONDLY ATTACHED, BA

We may, if we choose,
make the worst of one another.
Everyone has his weak points;
everyone has his faults;
we may make the worst of these;
we may fix our attention constantly upon these.
But we may also make the best of one another.
We may forgive, even as we hope to be forgiven.
We may put ourselves in the place of others,
and ask what we should wish to be done to us,
and thought of us, were we in their place,
by loving whatever is lovable in those around us.
Love will flow back from them to us,
and life will become a pleasure instead of a pain;
and earth will become like Heaven;
and we shall become not unworthy
followers of Him whose name is Love.

Our home joys
are the most delightful
earth affords,
and the joy of parents
in their children
is the most holy joy
of humanity.

There can can be no situation in life in which the conversation of my dear sister will not administer some comfort to me.

LADY MARY WORTLEY MONTAGU

In youth we learn; in age we understand.

Be devoted to one another in tender love.
ROMANS 12:10

Big sisters are the crab grass in the lawn of life.
CHARLES M. SCHULTZ

Sisters make the best friends because you always
know where they are. Friends may move and
you may lose contact with them. But with sisters,
it is comforting to know that the daily time you must
spend to keep up a friendship isn't as necessary
with a sister. For the love you've shared growing
up together, the memories that only you have,
and the understanding that comes from each of
your hearts makes it easy to pick up the pieces of the
last conversation, and go forward even though time
may have passed from the last time you talked.
RHONDA S. HOGAN

Because you love me, I have found
New joys that were not mine before;
New starts have lightened up my sky
With glories growing more and more.

Because you love me, I can rise
To the heights of fame and realms of power;
Because you love me, I may learn
The highest use of every hour.

Because you love me, I can choose
To look through your dear eyes and see
Beyond the beauty of the Now
Far onward to Eternity.

Because you love me, I can wait
With perfect patience well possessed;
Because you love me, all my life
Is circled with unquestioned rest.

Yes, even Life and even Death
Is all unquestioned and all blest.

AUTHOR UNKNOWN

The family is the essential presence—
the thing that never leaves you,
even if you find you have to leave it.

BILL BUFORD

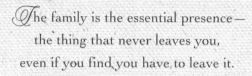

Our happiness in this world depends on the
affections we are enabled to inspire.

DUCHESE DE PRASLIN

Long may you live,
Happy may you be;
Loved by all,
But best by me.

Where you go I will go,
and where you stay I will stay.
Your people will be my people
and your God my God.
Where you die I will die,
and there I will be buried.
May the Lord deal with me,
be it ever so severely, if anything
but death separates you and me.

RUTH 1:16, 17

⌒⌒⌒⌒⌒⌒⌒

Only a sister can know the heart of a sister,
and the bonds of love.

Love much.

Earth has enough of bitter in it;
Cast sweets into its cup whene'er you can.
No heart so hard but love at last may win it.
Yes, love on through doubt and
darkness, and believe
There is nothing which love may not achieve.

ELLA WHEELER WILCOX

There is only one happiness in life,
to love and be loved.

GEORGE SAND

It Takes Two

The desire for friendship is strong
in every human heart. We crave the
companionship of those who understand.
The nostalgia of life presses, we sigh for "home,"
and long for the presence of one who
sympathizes with our aspirations,
comprehends our hopes, and is able to
partake of our joys. A thought is not
our own until we impart it to another
and the confessional seems to be a
crying need of every human soul.

A sister will
strengthen you
with her prayers,
bless you
with her love,
and encourage you
with her hope.